EXPLORING COUNTRIES

Canada

KAITE GOLDSWORTHY

D0010602

MEDIA ENHANCED BOOKS
AV2 BY WEIGL
ADDED VALUE • AUDIO VISUAL

www.av2books.com

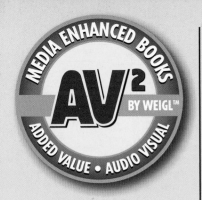

AV² provides enriched content that supplements and complements this book. Weigl's AV² books strive to create inspired learning and engage young minds in a total learning experience.

Your AV² Media Enhanced books come alive with...

Audio
Listen to sections of the book read aloud.

Key Words
Study vocabulary, and complete a matching word activity.

Video
Watch informative video clips.

Quizzes
Test your knowledge.

Go to **www.av2books.com**, and enter this book's unique code.

BOOK CODE

R 5 4 3 7 0 7

Embedded Weblinks
Gain additional information for research.

Slide Show
View images and captions, and prepare a presentation.

AV² by Weigl brings you media enhanced books that support active learning.

Try This!
Complete activities and hands-on experiments.

...and much, much more!

Published by AV² by Weigl
350 5ᵗʰ Avenue, 59ᵗʰ Floor
New York, NY 10118
Website: www.av2books.com   www.weigl.com

Library of Congress Cataloging-in-Publication Data

Goldsworthy, Kaite.
 Canada / Kaite Goldsworthy.
    p. cm. — (Exploring countries)
 Includes index.
 ISBN 978-1-62127-251-9 (hardcover : alk. paper) — ISBN 978-1-62127-257-1 (softcover : alk. paper)
 1. Canada—Juvenile literature. I. Title.
 F1008.2.G65 2013
 971—dc23   2012041014

Printed in the United States of America in North Mankato, Minnesota
1 2 3 4 5 6 7 8 9 17 16 15 14 13

052013
WEP040413

Project Coordinator Heather Kissock
Art Director Terry Paulhus

Photo Credits
Every reasonable effort has been made to trace ownership and to obtain permission to reprint copyright material. The publishers would be pleased to have any errors or omissions brought to their attention so that they may be corrected in subsequent printings.

Weigl acknowledges Getty Images as its primary image supplier for this title.

Contents

Canada Overview

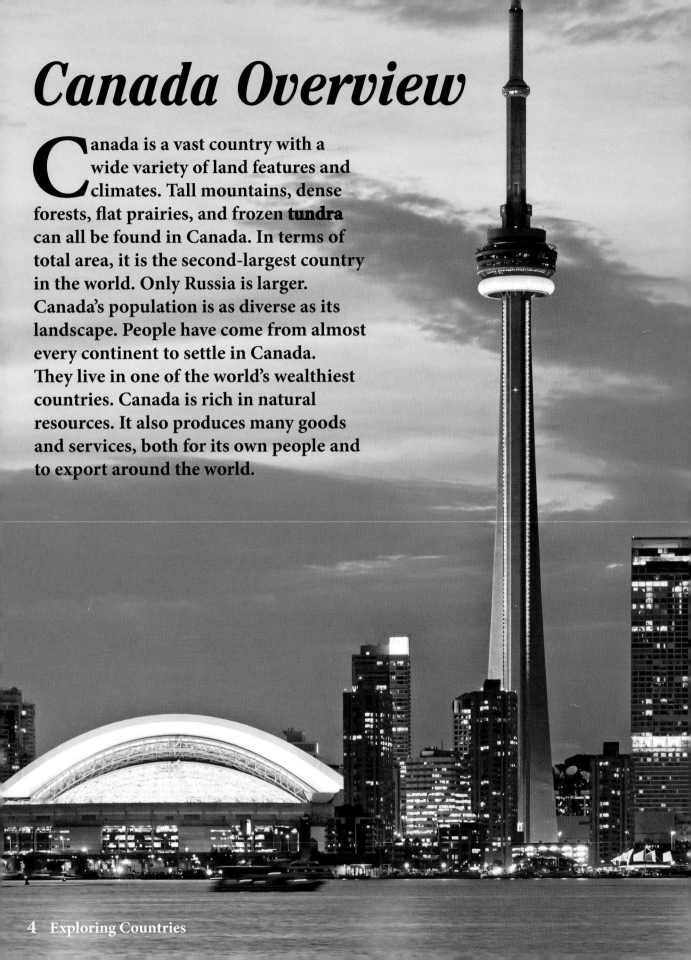

Canada is a vast country with a wide variety of land features and climates. Tall mountains, dense forests, flat prairies, and frozen **tundra** can all be found in Canada. In terms of total area, it is the second-largest country in the world. Only Russia is larger. Canada's population is as diverse as its landscape. People have come from almost every continent to settle in Canada. They live in one of the world's wealthiest countries. Canada is rich in natural resources. It also produces many goods and services, both for its own people and to export around the world.

Parliament Hill in Ottawa is the center of Canada's government. Most of its buildings were completed in the late 1800s and early 1900s.

Many signs in Canada are in both English and French.

The red maple leaf is Canada's national symbol. It can be seen on the red and white national flag.

People from many cultural backgrounds make up Canada's population, and represented their country at the 2012 Olympics.

The beaver is the national animal of Canada. Beavers can be found in lakes and streams in all parts of the country.

Exploring Canada

Canada is located in the northern part of the continent of North America. Its most northern point is only about 450 miles (725 kilometers) south of the North Pole. At its widest point, the country spans more than 3,400 miles (5,500 km) from east to west. It extends almost 2,900 miles (4,670 km) from north to south. Canada is bordered by the United States to the south. The U.S. state of Alaska borders Canada's Yukon territory and province of British Columbia on the west. Three oceans touch Canada's shores. They are the Pacific Ocean on the west, the Arctic Ocean on the north, and the Atlantic Ocean on the east.

Mount Logan

Vancouver Island

United States

Map Legend

Canada

Land

Water

Vancouver Island

Hudson Bay

Capital City

Mount Logan

500 Kilometers

SCALE

500 Miles

Vancouver Island

Located off the southwest coast of Canada, Vancouver Island has an area of more than 12,000 square miles (31,000 sq. km). One of Canada's largest islands, it includes mountains, lakes, forests, and beaches. It protects the mainland city of Vancouver from the Pacific Ocean, creating a calm-water harbor that makes the city a major seaport.

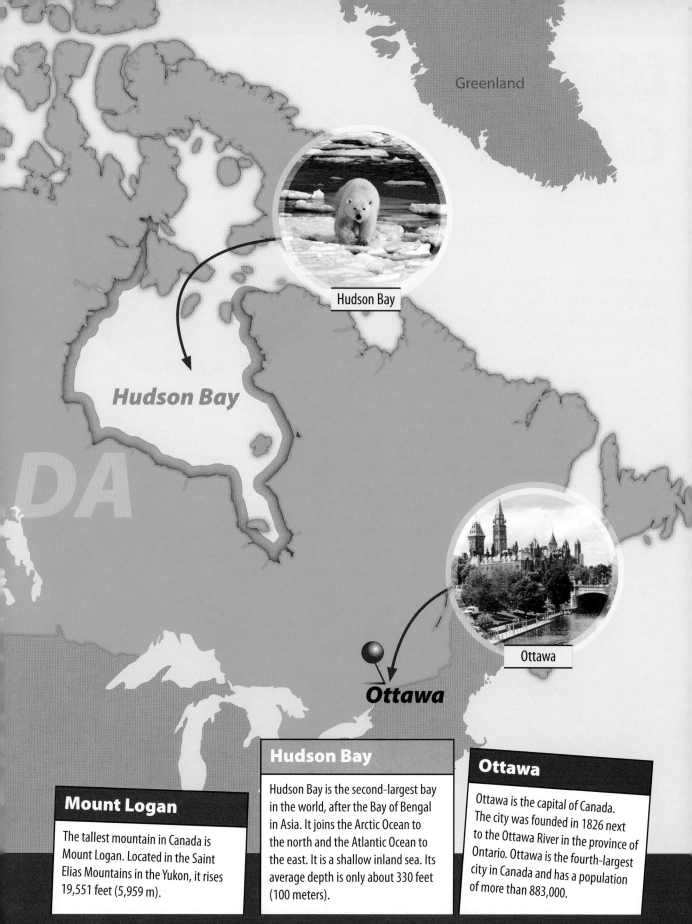

Greenland

Hudson Bay

Hudson Bay

DA

Ottawa

Ottawa

Mount Logan

The tallest mountain in Canada is Mount Logan. Located in the Saint Elias Mountains in the Yukon, it rises 19,551 feet (5,959 m).

Hudson Bay

Hudson Bay is the second-largest bay in the world, after the Bay of Bengal in Asia. It joins the Arctic Ocean to the north and the Atlantic Ocean to the east. It is a shallow inland sea. Its average depth is only about 330 feet (100 meters).

Ottawa

Ottawa is the capital of Canada. The city was founded in 1826 next to the Ottawa River in the province of Ontario. Ottawa is the fourth-largest city in Canada and has a population of more than 883,000.

LAND AND CLIMATE

Canada can be divided into several natural regions. The Atlantic region includes coastal lowlands and forests. The Mixedwood Plains cover the southern part of the province of Quebec and southeastern Ontario. This region was once mostly forests of evergreen and **deciduous** trees. Today, many cities and businesses occupy this area. The Boreal Shield stretches from the province of Newfoundland to the eastern edge of the province of Alberta in western Canada. Consisting of forests of evergreen trees, the Boreal Shield covers 20 percent of Canada.

Percé Rock is a unique natural land formation located near the mouth of the St. Lawrence River.

The Central Plains is a region of flat land that covers central Alberta and parts of the provinces of Saskatchewan and Manitoba. It has rich soil and is where most of Canada's wheat is grown. The Pacific and Western Mountains region includes mountains and **temperate rainforests**. The Arctic and Taiga regions make up most of northern Canada. These areas have the coldest climates found in Canada. The Arctic is a treeless tundra of mostly low-growing mosses, lichens, and hardy shrubs. The Taiga is largely wetlands with some spruce and fir trees.

There are eight different mountain ranges in Canada. The largest is the Rocky Mountains, which runs north-south through western Alberta and eastern British Columbia. South of Canada, the Rockies stretch through the western United States.

Close to 9 percent of Canada's landmass is covered by water. Most of this water is found in **glaciers** and thousands of lakes. Four of the five Great Lakes are partly in Canada. The country's major rivers include the Mackenzie and the St. Lawrence. The Mackenzie flows through northwestern Canada into the Arctic Ocean. The St. Lawrence, in eastern Canada, empties into the Atlantic. Overall, almost 7 percent of the world's fresh water supply can be found in Canada.

Canada is so large that the climate varies greatly across the country. Southern coastal areas generally have warmer, more humid climates than other regions. They receive more rain than snow during the winter months. Northern Canada has the coldest climate, especially regions in the Far North. Central Canada can have very warm summers but also very cold winters with a great deal of snow.

The Rocky Mountains in Alberta feature forests, valleys, mountains, glaciers, and numerous lakes and rivers.

Land and Climate BY THE NUMBERS

3,855,103
Total area of Canada in square miles. (9,984,670 sq. km)

SIX Number of time zones in Canada, including Newfoundland, Atlantic, Eastern, Central, Mountain, and Pacific Time.

150,993 miles
Length of Canada's coastline, which is the longest in the world. (243,000 km)

31,700
Approximate number of lakes in Canada.

PLANTS AND ANIMALS

Canada has many different **ecosystems**. They are home to more than 71,500 plant and animal **species**. Canada has 10 percent of the world's trees, and more than half the country is covered by forests. Most tree-covered land is boreal forest. This is a type of forest that has mostly **coniferous** trees, such as spruce, pine, and fir. Half of Canada's trees are spruce trees. Poplar, trembling aspen, white birch, and tamarack trees are also common.

The temperate rainforests on Canada's west coast are home to some of the tallest and oldest trees in Canada, including the western red cedar. The Rocky Mountains are covered in forests of coniferous trees. On the highest slopes, however, no trees can survive. The prairies in central Canada are a mix of grasslands and **bluffs** of trees, such as aspen. Eastern Canada has a wide variety of deciduous trees, including maple, hickory, oak, hemlock, and willow.

Two-thirds of Canada's wildlife species live in its forests, including beavers, lynx, and several types of deer. There are three species of bears in Canada, the brown bear, black bear, and polar bear. Polar bears can be found in Canada's northern regions. They are the largest bears in the world. Caribou, moose, wolves, arctic foxes, and muskoxen can also survive in northern Canada's colder climates.

The grizzly bear is a type of brown bear that lives in western Canada. An adult male can weigh between 400 and 700 pounds (180 and 320 kg).

Plants and Animals BY THE NUMBERS

1973
Year that Canada, the United States, Denmark, Norway, and the Soviet Union signed an agreement to protect the world's polar bears.

62 miles per hour
Running speed of the pronghorn, Canada's fastest animal. (100 km per hour)

90 pounds
Amount of food that a polar bear can eat in one meal. (40 kg)

8%
Portion of Canada's trees protected by special laws that say new trees must be planted when old trees are cut down.

NATURAL RESOURCES

Many different types of energy resources are found in Canada, including crude oil, natural gas, and coal. The Athabasca oil sands in Alberta contain the world's second-largest oil reserves. Overall, Canada is the fifth-largest energy producer in the world.

Good soil and climate conditions for growing crops and raising livestock make agriculture an important industry. The prairie provinces of Alberta, Saskatchewan, and Manitoba grow wheat and canola. Fruits and vegetables are grown in British Columbia's Okanagan Valley and the Niagara region of Ontario. The Maritime Provinces on Canada's east coast are known for their potatoes. These provinces are New Brunswick, Nova Scotia, and Prince Edward Island. Livestock commonly raised in Canada include cows, sheep, pigs, and chickens. Beef is an important agricultural product in Alberta.

Canada's rivers and forests are valuable resources. Dams on Canada's rivers are used to generate **hydroelectricity**. Logging is an important industry, especially in British Columbia, Ontario, and Quebec.

There are more than 200 mines in Canada. These mines produce more than 60 different types of metals and minerals, including copper, gold, zinc, lead, iron, and cobalt. Canada is one of the top-five producers of aluminum, cadmium, nickel, platinum, titanium, and salt.

$39 billion
Value of Canada's annual exports of agricultural products.

11%
Portion of the total goods and services produced in Canada that comes from mining, forestry, and oil and gas production.

15 YEARS
Length of time that the oil in the Athabasca oil sands could meet the energy needs of the entire world.

Canada is the biggest producer of canola. This crop is mostly used to make cooking oil, but canola oil is also used in fuel, ink, and fertilizer.

TOURISM

Many people visit Canada for its natural beauty. Canada has a national parks system that protects many scenic areas so that they can be enjoyed by people both today and in the future. Banff National Park in western Alberta, which covers more than 2,500 square miles (6,500 sq. km), is one of Canada's top tourist destinations. Established in 1885, it was the country's first national park. Today, more than 3 million people visit Banff each year. In the winter, many people enjoy downhill skiing and snowboarding in the Rockies, as well as in eastern Canada.

Beluga whales are a popular attraction at the Vancouver Aquarium.

The Bay of Fundy, on Canada's east coast, is an excellent spot for whale watching. The bay is also well known for having the highest tides in the world. Canada's west coast offers visitors the combined beauty of mountains and ocean views. The city of Vancouver, in British Columbia, is a popular destination for tourists. The Vancouver Aquarium gives visitors a chance to learn about the world's oceans and view more than 50,000 sea animals.

The Bow River flows through Banff National Park. Visitors can enjoy rafting or fishing surrounded by some of the most beautiful scenery in the world.

Niagara Falls attracts visitors from all over the world. Located on the border between Ontario and the U.S. state of New York, it is made up of three separate waterfalls. One of them, Horseshoe Falls, is on the Canadian side. It is the tallest of the three, with a height of 170 feet (50 m).

Quebec City is the capital of the largely French-speaking province of Quebec. In the center of the city is Old Quebec, or Vieux-Québec. Quebec was founded more than 400 years ago. It is the only place in North America north of Mexico with its original defensive walls still standing. The Chateau Frontenac is one of the most-photographed hotels in the world. It looks like a castle and is one of Old Quebec's main attractions.

Canada's capital city of Ottawa offers visitors the chance to visit Parliament Hill. Visitors can enjoy a beautiful view of Ottawa from the top of the Peace Tower. The National Gallery of Canada holds the largest collection of Canadian art in the country. Next door is the Royal Canadian Mint where visitors can see Canadian money being made. Ottawa has many museums to visit, such as the Museum of Nature, Canada Aviation and Space Museum, and Canadian War Museum.

INDUSTRY

Manufacturing is an important part of Canada's economy. The country has hundreds of factories that produce motor vehicles and auto parts. More than 2 million cars and trucks are made each year, and Canada is the sixth-largest vehicle exporter. Aircraft, agricultural machinery, and equipment used in the oil and gas industry are also made in Canada.

About 1.6 million Canadians have jobs related to natural resources. Energy resources are also one of the country's main exports. Canada is the second-largest exporter of forest products, such as timber and wood pulp. It is the world's biggest producer of newsprint paper. Another important export is potash, a type of fertilizer, which is mined mostly in Saskatchewan. The country has almost half the world's total potash reserves. Uranium mining is also important in Saskatchewan. Canada is one of the world's leading producers of uranium, which is used to generate electricity in nuclear power plants.

Canada's access to so many oceans, lakes, and rivers makes fishing an important industry. The country is the seventh-largest exporter of seafood, sending its products to more than 130 countries. Canada is known for snow crabs, lobsters, and Atlantic farmed salmon.

$6.7 BILLION
Value of Canada's potash exports in 2011.

15% Portion of Canada's electricity that is produced in nuclear power plants.

308,000
Number of Canadians employed in the mining industry.

The aerospace industry is a growing sector of Canada's economy. More than 80,000 people work in the manufacturing of aircraft and parts used to make planes.

GOODS AND SERVICES

4% Portion of the world's gold that is mined in Canada.

Canada has a **free trade agreement** with the United States and Mexico. This agreement allows the three countries to more easily import from and export to one another. Canada sends more than $300 billion worth of goods and services to the United States each year. This is almost three-quarters of Canada's total exports. Canada imports more than $280 billion worth of goods and services annually from the United States.

MORE THAN 100,000

Number of elementary and secondary schoolteachers in Canada.

Many imports and exports enter or leave Canada through the Great Lakes St. Lawrence Seaway System. This is a 2,340-mile (3,700-km) waterway that extends from the mouth of the St. Lawrence River, on the Atlantic coast, to the western end of the Great Lakes. Many canals and **locks** have been built at places that were difficult or impossible for ships to pass. As a result, large cargo ships can now travel into central North America.

17 Days Average time for a cargo ship to travel the Great Lakes St. Lawrence Seaway System from Thunder Bay, Ontario, to the mouth of the St. Lawrence River.

Although manufacturing, agriculture, and natural resources are all important to Canada's economy, a majority of Canadian workers now make their living in service industries. These are industries in which workers provide a service to other people, rather than produce goods. Service workers include people employed in schools and colleges, hospitals, banks, stores, hotels, and restaurants. People such as lawyers and software developers are also service workers.

Since the St. Lawrence Seaway opened in 1959, more than 2.7 billion tons (2.5 billion tonnes) of cargo have been shipped on this waterway.

INDIGENOUS PEOPLES

Many scientists believe the first people came to North America about 15,000 years ago, traveling from Asia to Alaska. Over time, their **descendants** spread out across North America. In Canada, there are three main groups of **indigenous** peoples, or Aboriginal Canadians. They are the First Nations, Inuit, and Métis peoples.

First Nations peoples traditionally lived across most of Canada. Different groups adapted their way of life to the resources of their regions. Those on the prairies were **nomadic**. They followed the bison herds, which they hunted. They used bison meat for food and bison hides to make their clothing and homes. Groups along the coasts lived in permanent settlements, fishing and hunting for food. Over time, many of these groups began farming. Today, the Canadian government recognizes more than 600 First Nations.

Inuit people, or Eskimos, traditionally lived in Canada's Far North. The Inuit survived by fishing and hunting animals such as seals, whales, and caribou. These animals provided food and clothing. Fat from whales and seals was used for fuel. Many Inuit still live in the smaller communities of northern Canada, especially in the territory of Nunavut.

Canada's Métis people are descended from First Nations people and early French fur traders and settlers. The Métis have their own distinct culture, which combines both French and First Nations traditions. The Métis language, Michif, is a blend of French and Cree. It is still spoken today.

1999 Year that the territory of Nunavut was established, in part to settle Inuit land claims against the Canadian government.

More Than 50 Number of different Aboriginal languages spoken in Canada.

2% Portion of Canada's population that is made up of First Nations peoples.

Totem poles were carved by many First Nations that lived along Canada's west coast.

THE AGE OF EXPLORATION

Around the year 1000 AD, Vikings became the first Europeans to reach Canada. Sailing from Greenland, they established a settlement at L'Anse aux Meadows on the island of Newfoundland. The settlement likely lasted for only a few years.

Beginning about 500 years later, a number of European explorers reached Canada. Many of the early explorers were looking for a way to sail to Asia. John Cabot arrived in 1497. Sailing for England, he mapped Canada's east coast. In 1534, French explorer Jacques Cartier landed in eastern Canada and claimed the region for France. Cartier helped to name the country after hearing his guides use the Iroquois word *kanata*, which means "village."

Explorers continued to come to Canada, and they were followed by fur traders. Beaver hats were popular in Europe during the 1600s, and Canada had a large beaver population at that time. Europeans would trade tools, pots, and other items to Canada's First Nations peoples. In return, they would receive beaver **pelts**. Explorers and traders began to map large areas of Canada. Most fur traders were French or English, and there was a great rivalry between them. Traders would bring their ships in and out of Hudson Bay, which became the center of the fur trade. Over time, a British company, the Hudson's Bay Company, gained control of most of this trade.

500,000
Estimated population of Aboriginal Canadians before the arrival of Europeans.

1608
Year the settlement of Quebec was founded by French explorer Samuel de Champlain.

1670 Year the Hudson's Bay Company was established.

L'Anse aux Meadows is a National Historic Site. It features a re-creation of some of the settlement's Viking buildings.

EARLY SETTLERS

I n the 1600s and 1700s, more and more French and English settlers came to Canada. Many settlements were created along the Atlantic coast, on the St. Lawrence River, and in other parts of eastern Canada. Both England and France claimed this region and established **colonies**.

France and England, which was part of Great Britain starting in the 1700s, fought several wars for control of the area. The last conflict was the French and Indian War, which began in 1754. Great Britain won the war seven years later. As a result, France lost most of its colonies, and Great Britain controlled almost all of eastern North America.

Explorers and fur traders helped open the way for the arrival of European settlers in Canada.

The French and Indian War was fought by regular French and British troops, as well as colonial militias and Aboriginal groups. The long and costly struggle ended with the signing of the Treaty of Paris in 1763.

Great Britain's 13 colonies south of Canada rebelled against British rule in 1775. They won their independence at the end of the American Revolution in 1783 and formed the United States of America. A number of American colonists who wanted to remain under British rule moved north to Canada at that time.

Disputes between Great Britain and the United States over trade led to the War of 1812. Several major battles were fought in Canada. The 1814 Treaty of Ghent that ended the war helped to set the borders between Canada and the United States.

In the 1800s, Great Britain's colonies in Canada gained more power to govern themselves. The British North America Act, which went into effect on July 1, 1867, joined several areas together in the **Confederation** of Canada. At first, the confederation included Ontario, Quebec, Nova Scotia, and New Brunswick. Other areas joined later.

Many settlers began to move into western Canada's prairies in the 1870s. Eastern Canada was starting to become crowded, and there was more land to farm in the west. To encourage settlement, the government created the Dominion Lands Act in 1872. The act gave free land to settlers if they stayed for three years and improved the property.

The act helped to attract more settlers. Many came from Europe and the United States, as well as from eastern Canada. Some people, such as Mennonites and Doukhbors from Russia, came to escape religious **persecution** in their home countries.

Early Settlers BY THE NUMBERS

1949
Year that Newfoundland joined the Confederation of Canada.

160 acres
Amount of land given to each settler under the Dominion Lands Act. (65 hectares)

1931
Year the British government officially declared Canada to be completely self-governing.

The treaty that ended the War of 1812 was signed in the city of Ghent, in Belgium.

POPULATION

Canada is a large country with a small population. About 35 million people live in Canada. On average, that is about 10 people per square mile of land (4 per sq. km). The average for the United States is 89 people per square mile (34 per sq. km).

Canada's people are not spread out evenly across the country. The three northern territories have the smallest populations. These territories are Nunavut, the Northwest Territories, and Yukon. More than 60 percent of Canadians live in the central provinces of Ontario and Quebec. Another 13 percent live in British Columbia. The Atlantic Provinces, which are the three Maritime Provinces plus Newfoundland and Labrador, have about 7 percent of Canada's population. The prairie provinces are home to 18 percent of Canada's people.

Almost seven out of ten Canadians live in urban areas. Toronto, in Ontario, is Canada's largest city, with more than 2.6 million people. Toronto's population is diverse. About half the people who move to Canada from other countries settle in the Toronto area. Montreal, in Quebec, is Canada's second-largest city, with 1.6 million people.

In recent years, Canada's population has been growing slowly. Most of the population growth has come from **immigration**. Many recent immigrants have moved to Canada from countries in Asia and Latin America. **Multiculturalism** is an important part of Canada's official government policy.

1.1 Million
Population of Calgary, Alberta, Canada's third-largest city.

200,000
Approximate number of immigrants who move to Canada each year.

5.9% Canada's rate of population increase from 2006 to 2011.

The Greater Toronto Area, which includes the city and suburbs around it, is home to more than 5 million people.

POLITICS AND GOVERNMENT

Canada is a federal state. This means that power is shared between a national government and the governments of smaller areas within the country. In Canada, there are three levels of government. The federal government is responsible for national and international issues, such as relations with other countries, defense, trade, and immigration. The provincial and territorial governments are responsible for health, education, highways and roads, and natural resources within each province or territory. Municipal governments are responsible for many of the same services, but only in one town or city.

The country is a democracy, and citizens elect the key people who run the government. Canada has a parliamentary system that is based on the British system of government. Canada's Parliament has three parts. They are the House of Commons, the Senate, and the sovereign, who is the king or queen of Great Britain.

The 308 members of the House of Commons are elected. Most new laws start in the House of Commons and must be passed by a majority vote. The law must then also be passed by the Senate, whose members are appointed. As a last step, the law receives royal ascent. This means that the governor general, who represents the sovereign in Canada, officially approves the bill. The most important political leader in Canada is the prime minister. He or she is the head of the political party that has the largest number of seats in the House of Commons.

10 AND 3

Number of provinces and territories in Canada.

NINE Number of judges, including a chief justice, on Canada's Supreme Court, the country's highest court.

105 Number of members of the Senate.

Queen Elizabeth II has been Canada's sovereign for more than 60 years.

CULTURAL GROUPS

People from more than 200 different cultural backgrounds live in Canada, though most Canadians have British, French, or Aboriginal ancestry. People of European ancestry from countries such as Germany, Italy, the Netherlands, and Ukraine can be found in Canada. Many groups settled in specific areas of the country. In the 1800s, a large number of Ukrainian and other Eastern European immigrants settled on the prairies to farm. The population of Ukrainian Canadians is still highest in that part of the country today.

The world's largest Easter egg can be found in Alberta. Called a *pysanka*, it is decorated with traditional Ukrainian folk designs.

Throughout Canada's history, new immigrants have come to find work. Many were seeking a better way of life. Laws in the late 1700s and early 1800s made slavery illegal in Canada. Before slavery became illegal in the United States in 1865, the Underground Railroad helped more than 30,000 African American slaves reach Canada to start new lives. The Underground Railroad was a network of people opposed to slavery who gave escaped slaves traveling north places to stay, food, and other help.

In Newfoundland and Labrador, many people trace their ancestry to immigrants from Ireland.

Some cultural groups had difficult beginnings in Canada. In the 1880s, thousands of immigrants arrived from China to work on the Canadian Pacific Railway, the country's first transcontinental railroad. After the railroad was completed, however, the Canadian government wanted to set limits on immigration from China. It began charging a "head tax" for every person from China who wanted to come to Canada.

The Acadians were descendants of settlers from France in the 1600s. They set up the colony of Acadia on Canada's east coast. In the 1750s, many Acadians were forced to leave eastern Canada. However, the provinces of New Brunswick, Prince Edward Island, and Nova Scotia still reflect the influence of the Acadians in language and culture.

More than 100 different languages are spoken in Canada. The country has two official languages, English and French. The majority of Canadians speak English as their first language. For almost one-quarter of Canadians, French is their first language. Almost one out of five Canadians speaks a different language, such as German, Italian, Dutch, Polish, Punjabi, Chinese, or Arabic. Cree is the most common Aboriginal language spoken in Canada.

More than three-quarters of Canadians are followers of a Christian faith. Nearly 4 percent follow the Jewish faith. Islam, the religion of Muslims, is one of the fastest-growing faiths in Canada. There are also many Hindus, Sikhs, and Buddhists.

Cultural Groups BY THE NUMBERS

40% Portion of Canada's population that is Roman Catholic.

1/2 Fraction of Canada's Sikh population that lives in British Columbia.

2% Portion of Canadians who are Muslim.

Vancouver has one of Canada's largest communities of people with Chinese ancestry.

ARTS AND ENTERTAINMENT

Canada has several national arts organizations, such as the National Gallery of Canada, the National Ballet of Canada, and the National Theatre School. The National Arts Centre in Ottawa works with performing artists in theater, classical music, and dance. It is bilingual and has programs in English and French. Ontario's Stratford Shakespeare Festival attracts performers and audiences from around the world.

Drums have traditionally been used by many First Nations peoples.

The arts and music of Canada reflect the country's diverse heritage. Different styles of music are especially popular in certain regions. The Atlantic Provinces have a tradition of Irish music and fiddle playing. Western music is popular in the prairie provinces, where ranching and farming are a part of life.

Music is a vital part of Aboriginal Canadian culture, dating back hundreds and even thousands of years. Dancing traditionally marked celebrations and special events. Throat singing is a unique style of singing performed in Canada's Inuit communities. It is often done by Inuit women.

The Green Gables House is a popular tourist attraction and the setting for the novel *Anne of Green Gables* by Lucy Maud Montgomery. Written in 1908, the book has sold more than 50 million copies and has been translated into more than a dozen languages.

The country's landscapes have inspired many Canadian artists. Painter Emily Carr is one of the best known. Her paintings often show the forests, totem poles, and scenery along Canada's west coast. These works of art hang in museums around the world. The Group of Seven was a group of Canadian artists famous for their landscapes. They painted in the 1920s and 1930s, at the same time as Emily Carr.

Canadian written literature began with the arrival of Europeans. Many early explorers kept journals and wrote about their adventures. Today, books by such Canadian authors as Margaret Atwood, Lucy Maud Montgomery, Farley Mowat, Douglas Coupland, and W. O. Mitchell are read by people around the world.

Many Canadian performers are well-known worldwide. Popular singers and songwriters include Carly Rae Jepsen, Avril Lavigne, Neil Young, Alanis Morissette, Joni Mitchell, Michael Bublé, Justin Bieber, and Céline Dion. Many Canadians have found success in film and television. Well-known actors include Jim Carrey, Rachel McAdams, Mike Myers, Keanu Reeves, Donald and Kiefer Sutherland, and Graham Greene. Actor William Shatner is best known as Captain Kirk from *Star Trek*.

Arts and Entertainment BY THE NUMBERS

1915 Year that one of the best-known poems about World War I, "In Flanders Fields," was written by Canadian Lieutenant Colonel John McCrae.

11 Number of Academy Awards won by the movie *Titanic*, directed by Canadian James Cameron.

More Than 400 Million
Number of YouTube views of Carly Rae Jepsen's "Call Me Maybe" video.

Justin Bieber's albums have sold more than 15 million copies, and he performs his music at concerts worldwide.

SPORTS

Ice hockey is the most popular sport in Canada. It is Canada's official national winter sport. Ice hockey involves two teams of six players each. Players wear ice skates and have long hockey sticks, which they use to pass a rubber hockey puck along the ice. Teams can score a goal by getting the puck past the goal tender, or goalie, and into the opposing team's net.

Early lacrosse sticks used by Aboriginal Canadians sometimes featured beautiful carving. The ball was often made of animal skin.

Canada has seven professional hockey teams that play in the National Hockey League (NHL). The other NHL teams are based in the United States but include many Canadian players. Canada's men's team has won eight Olympic gold medals in ice hockey, more than any other country in Olympic history. The Canadian women's team has won three gold medals since women's ice hockey became an Olympic sport in 1998. Many adults and children play ice hockey across Canada at local rinks and ponds.

The Montreal Canadiens and Toronto Maple Leafs have competed in the NHL since the 1920s.

Canada's official national summer sport is lacrosse. It is played by two teams of ten players each. Players use a small, hard ball and a wooden stick with a scoop net, called a crosse, at one end. The net is used to throw and catch the ball. Each team tries to put the ball in the other team's goal. Lacrosse began as a sport played by some of Canada's First Nations peoples more than 500 years ago. Over time, the game was introduced to Canadian settlers of European descent.

The Canadian Football League (CFL) is Canada's major professional football league. CFL football is very similar to professional football in the United States, although there are some differences in the rules. CFL teams compete each year for the Grey Cup. The championship game is televised and is Canada's biggest single sporting event.

Many Canadians take advantage of the climate to enjoy a variety of winter sports. Both cross-country and downhill skiing are popular, as is snowboarding. Curling, a sport played on ice, is also popular in Canada. At other times of year, Canadians enjoy sports such as soccer, basketball, and baseball.

Sports BY THE NUMBERS

1891 Year that basketball was invented by Canadian James Naismith while he was working at a YMCA in Massachusetts.

ONE The Toronto Blue Jays are the only Canadian team in Major League Baseball.

24 Number of times that the Montreal Canadiens have won the Stanley Cup, the NHL's championship trophy.

Popular destinations for skiers and snowboarders include Mont Tremblant and other resorts in Quebec.

Mapping Canada

We use many tools to interpret maps and to understand the locations of features such as cities, states, lakes, and rivers. The map below has many tools to help interpret information on the map of Canada.

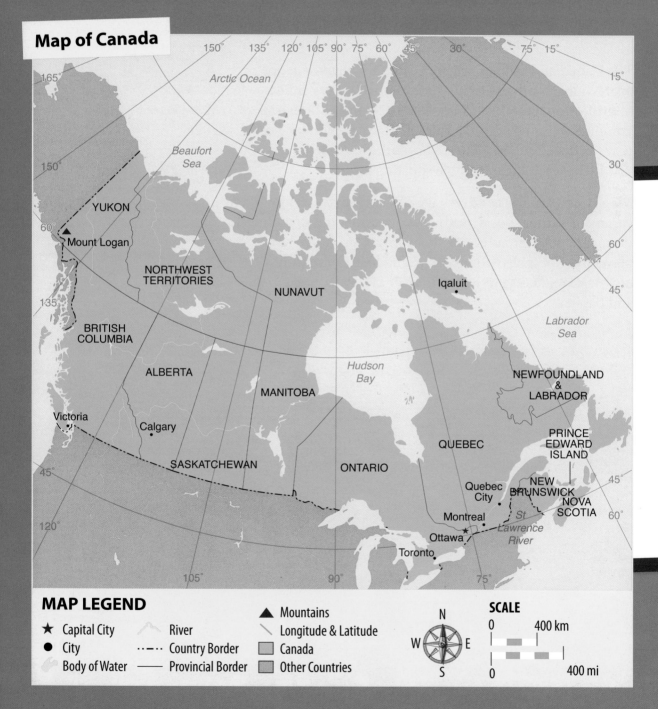

Map of Canada

Arctic Ocean

Beaufort Sea

YUKON

Mount Logan

NORTHWEST TERRITORIES

NUNAVUT

Iqaluit

Labrador Sea

BRITISH COLUMBIA

ALBERTA

Hudson Bay

NEWFOUNDLAND & LABRADOR

MANITOBA

Victoria

Calgary

SASKATCHEWAN

ONTARIO

QUEBEC

PRINCE EDWARD ISLAND

Quebec City

NEW BRUNSWICK

NOVA SCOTIA

Montreal

St Lawrence River

Ottawa

Toronto

MAP LEGEND

★ Capital City
● City
Body of Water
River
·–·– Country Border
—— Provincial Border
▲ Mountains
Longitude & Latitude
Canada
Other Countries

SCALE

0   400 km

0   400 mi

N W E S

Mapping Tools

- The compass rose shows north, south, east, and west. The points in between represent northeast, northwest, southeast, and southwest.
- The map scale shows that the distances on a map represent much longer distances in real life. If you measure the distance between objects on a map, you can use the map scale to calculate the actual distance in miles or kilometers between those two points.

- The lines of latitude and longitude are long lines that appear on maps. The lines of latitude run east to west and measure how far north or south of the equator a place is located. The lines of longitude run north to south and measure how far east or west of the Prime Meridian a place is located. A location on a map can be found by using the two numbers where latitude and longitude meet. This number is called a coordinate and is written using degrees and direction. For example, the city of Los Angeles would be found at 34°N and 118°W on a map.

Map It!

Using the map and the appropriate tools, complete the activities below.

Locating with latitude and longitude

1. What province is located at 46°N and 66°W?
2. What mountain is located at 60°N and 140°W?
3. What city can be found at 43°N and 79°W?

Distances between points

4. Using the map scale and a ruler, calculate the approximate distance between Montreal and Calgary.
5. Using the map scale and a ruler, calculate the approximate length of Labrador's coastline.
6. Using the map scale and a ruler, calculate the approximate length of the border between the provinces of Saskatchewan and Alberta.

Quiz Time

Test your knowledge of Canada by answering these questions.

1 Which Canadian city is more than 400 years old?

2 Which animal found in Canada can run more than 60 miles (100 km) an hour?

3 What is the only country larger in area than Canada?

4 How long is the Canadian coastline?

5 What is the capital of Canada?

6 How many waterfalls make up Niagara Falls?

7 What are Canada's national summer and winter sports?

8 How many different types of bears live in Canada?

9 What are the official languages of Canada?

10 Who is the most important political leader in Canada?

ANSWERS

1. Quebec
2. The pronghorn
3. Russia
4. 150,993 miles (243,000 km)
5. Ottawa
6. Three
7. Lacrosse and ice hockey
8. Three
9. English and French
10. The prime minister

Key Words

bluffs: groups of trees in a treeless area
colonies: lands outside its borders that a country claims and governs
confederation: a union of provinces, countries, or groups
coniferous: evergreen trees and shrubs that have cones
deciduous: trees that lose their leaves every year in a certain season
descendants: people who share common ancestors
ecosystems: communities of living things and resources
free trade agreement: an agreement that reduces the tariffs, or taxes and fees, countries pay when they trade goods
glaciers: large slow-moving sheets of ice

hydroelectricity: electricity produced using the energy of moving water, such as in a river
immigration: moving to a new country or area to live and work
indigenous: native to a particular area
locks: devices to raise or lower boats to different water levels
multiculturalism: respect and equal treatment for people from different cultural backgrounds
nomadic: related to a people who move around in search of food, water, and other needs
pelts: the skin and fur of animals that has been removed

persecution: to treat someone badly because of such things as the person's cultural group or religious beliefs
species: groups of individuals with common characteristics
temperate rainforests: forests that receive a great deal of rain or snow but that have cooler climates than tropical rainforests
tundra: flat land in which soil below the surface is always frozen and only small plants can grow
UNESCO: the United Nations Educational, Scientific, and Cultural Organization, whose main goals are to promote world peace and eliminate poverty through education, science, and culture

Index

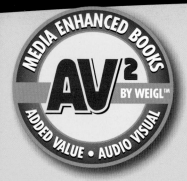

Log on to www.av2books.com

AV² by Weigl brings you media enhanced books that support active learning. Go to www.av2books.com, and enter the special code found on page 2 of this book. You will gain access to enriched and enhanced content that supplements and complements this book. Content includes video, audio, weblinks, quizzes, a slide show, and activities.

AV² Online Navigation

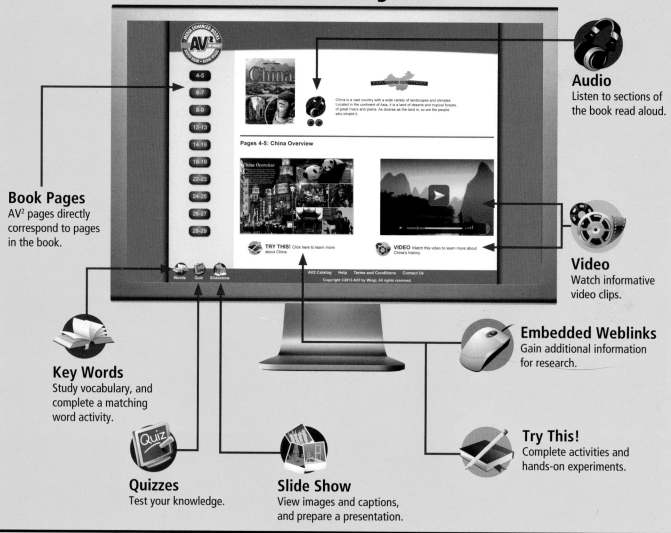

Book Pages
AV² pages directly correspond to pages in the book.

Audio
Listen to sections of the book read aloud.

Video
Watch informative video clips.

Embedded Weblinks
Gain additional information for research.

Key Words
Study vocabulary, and complete a matching word activity.

Try This!
Complete activities and hands-on experiments.

Quizzes
Test your knowledge.

Slide Show
View images and captions, and prepare a presentation.

AV² was built to bridge the gap between print and digital. We encourage you to tell us what you like and what you want to see in the future.

Sign up to be an AV² Ambassador at www.av2books.com/ambassador.

Due to the dynamic nature of the Internet, some of the URLs and activities provided as part of AV² by Weigl may have changed or ceased to exist. AV² by Weigl accepts no responsibility for any such changes. All media enhanced books are regularly monitored to update addresses and sites in a timely manner. Contact AV² by Weigl at 1-866-649-3445 or av2books@weigl.com with any questions, comments, or feedback.